AUTHOR'S NOTE

The theme of this book centers around a young boy who is quarantined in his bedroom because he has an infectious disease and, during that quarantine, is befriended by an extraordinary ant. Parents and doctors who come into the boy's room need to wear masks and surgical gloves to prevent becoming infected. I drafted this story a few years ago, before the Coronavirus pandemic began, but its progression to publication was delayed because of my primary career. In addition to writing, I'm also a lawyer. In the time between the draft of this book and its publication, I was involved in a lengthy and complex trial and other legal matters. I hope you enjoy the story I have created, and that it might bring a smile to children during this trying time."

— John Sharer

ANTS DON'T TALK, DO THEY?

BY JOHN SHARER
Illustrated by Jay Mazhar

ANTS DON'T TALK, DO THEY?

Published by Wompetias Press

Copyright © 2017, 2020 by John Sharer

Illustrations by Jay Mazhar

First Edition, 2020

All rights reserved.
This book may not be reproduced in whole or in part, in any form (beyond copying permitted by Sections 107 and 108 of the United States Copyright Law, and except limited excerpts by reviewer for the public press), without written permission from John Sharer.

Author services by Pedernales Publishing, LLC.
www.pedernalespublishing.com

ISBN 978-0-9961142-1-9 Hardcover edition
ISBN 978-0-9961142-0-2 Paperback edition
ISBN 978-0-9961142-2-6 Digital edition

Library of Congress Control Number: 2020908770

Printed in the United States of America

INTRODUCTION

This is a story about a lonely boy who had to stay in his room all by himself, all day every day for months, because the illness he had was contagious. He would get better but it would take time—a lot of time. One day, to keep himself busy and to take his mind off his loneliness, he was playing a game on his tablet. In the middle of the game, a real-life ant walked across the screen. It looked like a plain, ordinary ant, just like all the others the boy had seen in the garden and sometimes in the house. But the boy discovered, over the weeks that followed, that this was no ordinary ant. It did wondrous and seemingly magical things, and yet it was always kind and gentle and really helped the boy to overcome his loneliness and to get well.

CHAPTER ONE
THE MASKS

Chet hadn't felt all that sick, but he wasn't feeling all that well, either. He wasn't as hungry as he usually was. He was very tired, although he hadn't really done anything, and he had a bit of a fever. He figured something was going on when the doctors at the hospital were whispering together in a corner of the big room and looking at him from time to time. He quickly realized that it wasn't just the flu when they checked him into a room in the hospital. He stayed there for several days, and everybody who came into his room wore masks and gloves.

At first, not seeing anyone's face was scary, but after a while he got used to it. In fact, he played a little game, trying to place the name with the voice. It was easy when it was his father or mother and it became easy with his family doctor, Miguel Garcia. With nurses and other people in the hospitals, it was a bit harder. When the nurses realized he was no longer scared, they played along with the game by changing their voices to try to fool him. They fooled him for a while but not for long. The doctors at the hospitals were not as willing to play games. They were much more serious about what they were doing, although they and the nurses were always kind and gentle.

Doctor Garcia told Chet's parents and Chet that what he had wasn't too serious but it was very contagious—or as the doctor explained, catching—and when Chet went home from the hospital he would have to stay in his room twenty-four hours a day every day until he was better. The only people who could come and see him were his parents and the doctor. When they came to see him, they would have to wear masks and gloves. Doctor Garcia said that there was a medical breakthrough in the works that might be available very soon and would shorten the length of Chet's illness. Even without the breakthrough, the illness would be completely cured after two or three months. Until that time, he had to have all his meals in his room and he couldn't come out for any reason.

When he was released from the hospital, the faces reappeared without masks, but not in person. Chet's mother had made sure he had a phone, a television, a tablet, and his computer in his room. He could call his friends and they could call him. On the phone and on his tablet and computer he could see who he was talking to without them wearing a mask. This included his parents and his sister, Amelia, or whoever was in the house. His mother came into his room several times a day all masked and gloved, bringing him his meals, clean clothes, towels, toothpaste, and games. As instructed by Dr. Garcia, she didn't stay long and didn't touch Chet, even with gloves. He told her that, despite the protective clothing, there was always a risk of being infected.

He attended his classes online. He could see and hear the teacher and all the other students, and they could hear him but not see him. He got homework assignments just like he was actually in the classroom. He would complete the assignments and send them to school using the computer.

Although he was in his room or his bathroom twenty-four hours a day, he could connect to his teachers, his friends, and his family. He could see them and, except for his teachers, they could see him. He could watch TV and get onto the internet. He could send and get messages on his devices. He could play the many computer games he had. Despite all of this, he was lonely. He missed being free to leave his room, to go out on the street, and to walk to the store, to the park where he played touch football and soccer with his friends, and even to school to sit in classrooms.

But he missed one thing perhaps more than all the rest put together. Except for when he went to camp in the summer, his mother had kissed him goodnight and given him a hug at bedtime every day of his life. He had taken those loving moments for granted. His illness had taught him many things. One was not to take things for granted.

CHAPTER TWO
GOOD NEWS AND BAD NEWS

Dr. Garcia's next visit brought good and bad news. The hoped-for medical breakthrough that would have shortened Chet's illness would not be available for another year. On the other hand, Chet's blood tests showed that his infection was on the lower side, meaning he could perhaps be over the illness closer to two months than three.

Chet was able to see some good news and some bad news too, but not about cures, medicines, and the like. The bad news was the boredom and the isolation, even though he had all the electronic connections, they were not real substitutes for going out, playing with his friends, and even going to school. But he could sleep late; he wasn't getting wakened by his mom, dressing, rushing through breakfast and running to get the school bus. He could go to school in his pajamas. He could see and hear the teacher and the kids and they could hear him, but they couldn't see him. He felt strange being "in class" in his pajamas, but he found it funny. He ate a banana in English class, a real no-no, and during a particularly boring math class he played Fortnite. Sometimes he would play soccer games on his computer. His favorite player was Lionel Messi and his favorite team was Chelsea. He would only play these games once in a while during school, and he would keep listening to the teacher in case he was called on. None of these "bad things" were ever found out by his teachers and he never had to stay after school, go to the principal's office, or take a note home to his parents, even if he could have.

As he got used to his isolation, he began to accept it and even enjoy it, although not all that much. He got lots of calls and messages from his friends.

"Hey Chet, you want to play chess?" Jack Williams was a good friend. Both of them were members of the newly formed chess club at school.

"Sure, set 'em up." They played on Skype so they could both watch the board that Jack had set up at his house. They played every evening after school for a week or so. Sometimes they played two games. Once they played three.

Ray Simpson called one Saturday morning. "Chet, how you doing? Jim and Ramon are over at my house. We're going to watch the Lakers play the Celtics on TV. It starts in five minutes. You always liked both of those teams. Why don't you turn it on in your house? It'll be like we're all watching it in the same room." Chet did that and it really felt like they were all in the same room. They sent each other messages during the game and had a joint phone call afterward, arguing whether the winning score should have been goal-tending and why time-out wasn't called with three seconds left.

Afterward, Ramon said, "Hey, that was fun. Let's do this again only let's change the sport. Chelsea is playing Manchester United in soccer tomorrow and it'll be on TV. The three us will be at my house and we know where you'll be, Chet. Okay?" Everybody agreed, but everyone but Chet found something else to do and Chet watched the game alone.

There were lots of calls, lots of texts, and lots of "how you doing?" and "when are you going to be able to leave your room?" But as the weeks went by, there were fewer messages, fewer phone calls, fewer games to watch and fewer chess matches. It was not a lack of caring, but the novelty had worn off, and slowly the friends returned to their typical after-school and weekend activities, playing football and soccer, going to the beach, and just hanging out. Things that Chet couldn't do, at least not for a while.

CHAPTER THREE
THE ARRIVAL OF THE ANT

It was spring break. Some of his friends went away with their parents for the two weeks. Some went to camp and some just hung out. There was no school to connect with on his computer and the contacts with his friends, which had come less often over the weeks, dried up almost completely. He had some books in his room but he had read most of them. The ones he hadn't read, he didn't like. He loved playing computer games, but even that got old after a while. There was no sports on TV, and he wasn't interested in daytime sitcoms. He decided to log on to his computer and see if there was anything interesting. He scrolled through some sites but didn't find anything he wanted to read or watch. He was about to log out when a very small ant walked slowly across the screen.

"Hello," said Chet, "what are you doing on my screen?" He was so anxious to find something to do that he was even ready to talk to an ant.

"Hey ant, you know something? I'm stuck in this room. Can't leave. Not for a long time. What about you? I bet you could go anywhere you wanted. Probably take you a week to get there, but you could climb down off that screen and go under the door, down the stairs and out in the garden. You'd probably find some good stuff to eat and maybe some other little ants like you."

Just then his mother came in with his lunch.

"Who are you talking to?"

"An ant."

"Which aunt–Sally, Jane, or Betty? If it's Aunt Betty, don't hang up. I've got to ask her something."

"Not A-U-N-T. I'm talking to an A-N-T."

"You're talking to a what?"

"I'm talking to an ant, a tiny insect who is visiting me and is right now on my computer screen."

"Are you feeling all right? Do you have a fever? Maybe I should call Dr. Garcia."

"I'm fine. I'm feeling all right. I don't have a fever. I didn't have anyone else to talk to and the ant listens good."

"He listens 'well,' not 'good.'"

"Yes he does. I'm glad you noticed that. I called him 'he' but maybe he's a she. I don't think you can tell with ants."

"I'm going to call Dr. Garcia."

"Why? Talking to animals isn't that weird. You talk to our dog, Lily. I've heard you. People talk to their dogs and cats all the time. Grandpa talks to his pet bird. Nobody thinks they'll answer, but nobody thinks it's crazy to talk to animals."

"Talking to dogs, cats, and birds is different."

"Why is it different? An ant is an animal just like a dog, only smaller. I bet this ant is a lot smarter than any dog or cat. You don't have to take an ant out to poo like you have to do with a dog. You don't have to take an ant to the vet to get rid of a hair ball like a cat who swallows its own hair."

Although she called, Dr. Garcia did not come to see Chet or call him that day. Apparently, he thought Chet was fine too.

CHAPTER FOUR
AN INSECT NAMED SIR RUFUS ANT

The first thing Chet did every morning when he woke up was to log on to his computer and look for the ant. Sometimes the ant was on the screen, walking or crawling (or whatever it is that tiny ants do to get from one place to another). Sometimes it was not there but would appear later. Every once in a while, it would go to the edge of the computer and disappear and then come back an hour or so later. Where he went during those times was a mystery.

Chet didn't know much about ants. In his third grade class, they had talked a lot about animals. They even talked about some insects, like bees, who made honey, and cockroaches, who were some of the oldest living things in the world. But they never talked about ants. He got his encyclopedia down from the bookshelf and looked up ants. There was a lot of technical stuff that he breezed by, but there was also some interesting stuff.

The most interesting thing he read was that they communicated with each other by sound and touch. Since there was only one ant on his screen, he couldn't check the touch thing, but he could check the sound. When the ant reappeared, Chet put his ear as close to the ant as he could without actually touching him—

nothing. He said loudly, "Say something"—nothing. Maybe ants only talked to other ants. There weren't any others around, so he drew a small ant on a piece of paper, carefully cut it out, and placed it close to the ant—nothing. Chet figured that maybe the ant was shy and hadn't got used to him yet. Either that or the ant was too smart to be fooled by a pretty bad drawing.

"If we're going to be friends and we're going to be talking to each other, or at least I'll be talking to you, I can't just call you 'ant.' I thought about 'Itsy Bitsy Ant,' sorta like itsy bitsy spider, but that's kinda childish. I'm going to call you 'Rufus,' although maybe 'Ruth' would be more proper. Better yet, I'll call you 'Sir Rufus Ant,' like the knights of the Round Table or the ones in Robin Hood or Ivanhoe."

Chet watched the ant for a long time, maybe an hour or more. It would walk a straight line, then suddenly turn right or left, then circle or go back the way it had come. There seemed to be no sense to its movements. Maybe it was practicing going out for a pass, getting ready for the ants versus spiders football game. Or maybe it had gotten into an open wine bottle in the kitchen and was drunk.

Then a funny thing happened. The screen was open to a story that Chet had been reading. Sir Rufus walked across the screen and set one of his six little legs on the letter H. He stayed there for about ten seconds, perhaps to let Chet realize that he was starting a message. Rufus then walked a little further and put another of his legs on the letter I, then he walked to the edge of the screen and disappeared.

"Wait a minute, Sir Rufus. Don't go. You only put a foot on an H and an I. Finish the message. There's got to be more."

Chet sat down and thought for a moment. "That wasn't a message. He's just a dumb ant. He could have stopped on any letter. He wasn't sending a message."

Chet thought some more. "Wait a minute. H and I spell 'Hi.' He was saying hello to me!"

"If we're going to be friends and we're going to be talking to each other, or at least I'll be talking to you, I can't just call you 'ant.' I thought about 'itsy bitsy' ant sorta like itsy bitsy spider but that's kinda childish. I'm going to call you 'Rufus' although maybe 'Ruth' would be more proper. Better yet, I'll call you Sir Rufus Ant like the knights of the Round Table or those in Robin Hood or Ivanhoe."

Chet watched the ant for a long time; maybe an hour or more. It would walk a straight line then suddenly turn right or left, then circle or go back the way it had come. There seemed to be no sense to its movements. Maybe it was practicing going out for a pass getting ready for the ants versus spiders football game or

Just at that moment, his mother came in.

"Mom, Rufus sent me a message. He said Hi."

"Who's Rufus? Is he a friend from school? I never heard you talk about any Rufus."

"Mom, he's not a friend from school. He's the ant I told you about. He knows English."

"Don't be ridiculous. Ants don't know English. I'm going to get a tissue and flush that ant down the toilet."

"No, Mom. Please don't. I won't say anything about him again."

"Well okay, but do something sensible. Watch a TV show, or better yet, read a book."

CHAPTER FIVE
SIR RUFUS TALKS

Sir Rufus hadn't been around for several days following the 'Hi' message, or non-message. When first waking up, Chet would be eager to see Sir Rufus. As the days went by without the ant appearing, Chet started to believe that Sir Rufus was just an ant who had wandered onto his computer, that it had no ability to talk to people, and that it had finally wandered off somewhere that ants wandered off to. Maybe the ant that he saw from time to time wasn't even the same one. Maybe it wasn't a boy ant at all. There was no way he could distinguish one ant from another. Ants weren't thin or fat, tall or short. They just all looked exactly the same as each other.

The ant chapter was over and so were the spring holidays. His friends who had left town with their parents were back. School had started up again. It had been a month since Chet had first been quarantined in his room, and Dr. Garcia was even more confident that Chet would be totally cured in one more month and could then leave his room and end his isolation. Memories of the ant faded and were replaced with increased contact with friends and with schoolwork. He had a nightly chess game with Jack Wilson on Skype and watched Chelsea playing in the semifinals of the FA Cup in his room while his friends Ray Simpson and Ramon Martinez watched at Ramon's house. They talked for an hour afterward about the game and a lot of other stuff.

"Hey Chet. Wake up. Forgot all about me, have you? Well I didn't forget about you. I had some things to take care of, but I'm back."

Chet leaped out of bed. He had been fast asleep, but he was now wide awake. "Who's there? Where are you?"

"It's me. Sir Rufus Ant."

"Don't kid me. Who are you and where are you?"

"I told you. It's your favorite ant, and I'm right here on your computer."

"It's Danny, Danny Gibson playing his tricks. I know it's you. You've put some kind of microphone or speaker somewhere in this room."

"Look around. See anything like that? Don't forget to look under the bed and in the closets. Maybe it's in your underwear drawer. Perhaps it's in the bathroom. Look in the shower."

Chet opened all the drawers in his room, crawled under the bed, pulled the cushions off the chairs, looked under the pictures and searched the bathroom, even turning the shower on in case something was hidden there. It was all silly. Even if Danny or anyone else wanted to plant a microphone, how could they do that without him knowing, unless he was fast asleep? And he would have woken up anyway.

"Didn't find anything, did you? Now log on to your tablet and tell me where you can see an ant on the screen."

Chet looked carefully and said, "In the upper right corner of the screen."

"All right. Now watch carefully. I'm going to walk to the dead center of the screen." And he did.

"Now, can Danny or anyone else create that? No. Not even Albert Einstein. Now go take a shower, have your breakfast, and go to school, and I'll be back later today and we'll have a nice chat." With that, Sir Rufus walked to the edge of the screen and disappeared.

CHAPTER SIX
THE PSYCHIATRIST

"Mom, I talked to Sir Rufus Ant just now."

"Back during spring break you told me you talked to him and I told you I was going to talk to Dr. Garcia and for you to watch TV or read a book and forget that nonsense."

"Yes, but now it's different. Sir Rufus talked to me. He's coming back after school to talk some more."

"All right. We'll just see. When he comes back, you call me. If I hear him talking, we'll both go to the loony bin. Maybe they have a special—two for the price of one. Seriously Chet, no joking. You've got to stop making up these weird stories."

"Just wait and see."

The school day seemed to go on forever. Chet was anxious that his parents hear Sir Rufus. He could hardly wait. Later that evening, Sir Rufus appeared on the computer screen.

"I'm back, Chet. What do you want to talk about? Maybe we could play a game. I know some real good ones."

"Wait, Sir Rufus, I want my parents to hear you. They think I made it all up."

"They won't be able to hear me, Chet. Only you can."

"I hear you real clear. They will too." Chet called his parents on their tablet downstairs. "Mom, Dad, come up here. Hurry."

His parents ran up the stairs. "What's wrong? What's happened? Are you feeling bad?"

"I'm fine. I want you to listen to Sir Rufus." He turned to the ant. "Say something to my parents."

"I told you, Chet, that only you can hear me. Your parents are very nice people and you're lucky to have them, but they won't be able to hear me. That's just the way it has to be."

"Dad, Mom, you heard that, didn't you?"

"We didn't hear anything and neither did you. We know it's tough for you, having to stay in this room all by yourself. But it won't be much longer, and if it makes the time go faster for you to make up a talking ant, then fine."

But neither parent actually thought it was fine, and they arranged through Dr. Garcia for Chet to see a child psychiatrist.

Dr. Emily Stern spent an hour in a video conference with Chet. She asked him a lot of questions both about Sir Rufus and about a lot of other stuff. She hadn't planned to spend that much time with Chet but she found him to be a very bright and very pleasant child. She enjoyed the time she spent with him.

Later, in a video conference with Chet's parents, she gave them the results of her examination.

"That boy is as sane as I am. Maybe more so. You have nothing to worry about."

"But what about him believing that an ant is talking to him? Doesn't sound rational."

"It's perfectly rational and quite normal, particularly for a child who is isolated and lonely. I'm sure you've heard of children having imaginary friends. Don't tell anyone, but I had one when I was a little younger than Chet."

"Aren't imaginary friends supposed to be make-believe children, not make-believe insects?"

Dr. Stern thought for a moment. "I can't say I've ever heard of a child having a make-believe insect friend, but it doesn't strike me as a problem."

"Okay, but this insect is not imaginary. It's sitting there right on his computer screen. What is imaginary is the idea that it can talk."

"Not to worry. Dr. Garcia told me that Chet will be free of his illness in a month or less. I predict that once he is able to leave his room and go back to his normal life, outside playing with his friends and physically back in school, he'll be finished with his make-believe friend. In the meantime, don't be angry with him about the friend. It will pass and he'll be fine."

As she sat in her office, Dr. Stern went over her conversation with Chet about his make-believe friend. Chet's description of the ant's conduct and what they talked about, along with Chet's obvious intelligence, made her think that maybe, just maybe, it wasn't so make-believe after all. She decided she had better keep that to herself.

CHAPTER SEVEN
SIZE AND SOUND

It had not been a great day. School was more boring than usual. Dr. Garcia had come by in the late afternoon and had given Chet a shot and had brought some awful-tasting medicine that he had to take three times a day for a week. However, things picked up in the evening. Sir Rufus came by and taught Chet a new song. He loved it and they sang it together three times. When they were tired of singing, Sir Rufus taught Chet a new game called Rontoona. Chet said he'd never heard of it.

"It was invented and played in a small South Pacific island more than a thousand years ago. That island disappeared two or three hundred years later, and so did the game. There's no record of it anywhere. You won't find any mention of it in any history book or encyclopedia or anywhere else."

"How did you know about it?"

"I can't tell you everything, at least not all at once."

Chet loved the game and pretty soon got to be good at it. He even beat Sir Rufus twice, although he thought that perhaps Sir Rufus had let him win.

Chet said that a couple of things were on his mind. "You know when I'm across the room and you say something, I have a hard time hearing you. I wouldn't want to make you shout and maybe hurt your throat."

"Not to worry. I can raise my voice to any level. I can make it so that people who live three or four blocks away could hear me clearly if I wanted them to. Of course, I don't want to scare the neighbors, so only you will hear me."

"Another thing, and I don't want to hurt your feelings, but you're so little that sometimes I can't see you when I'm not real close."

"That's no problem, either. I can make myself as big as this house or even as big as the Empire State Building. I did that once, just to see if I could, but there's never a reason for me to get that big. But I've often made myself a bit bigger so that children can see me better, especially those who have eye trouble. Here, let me show you."

With that, Sir Rufus very slowly grew in size until he was about twelve inches tall.

"What do you think of that! Can you see me and hear me better?"

"Wow that's great!"

The door suddenly opened and Chet's mother walked in.

"Mom, look at Sir Rufus. Look at how big he is."

"What, more nonsense about a silly insect? I don't see any ant."

"He's right there on the table, next to the lamp. Don't you see him?"

She peered at the area Chet had indicated.

"I don't have my glasses. I see a tiny little blur. Could be an ant or a speck of dust."

"But he's not tiny. He's a foot high."

"Don't be ridiculous. No ant is a foot high. Here's a glass of milk. Take it with your medicine. By the way, what was that song you were singing? I never heard you sing it before."

"If I told you that Sir Rufus taught it to me you'd just laugh, so I'll say I heard it on the TV."

After his mother left, Chet said, "I'll bet you're going to tell me that I am the only one who can see that you've grown twelve inches."

"You're right. You're learning. How about another game of Rontoona?"

CHAPTER EIGHT
CHET AND AMELIA

Chet had a sister, Amelia, who was two years older than Chet. He would talk to her on his tablet. On school days they usually talked only once, but on weekends they talked two or three times.

"Chet, why won't Sir Rufus let Mom and Dad hear him talk?" Unlike their father and mother, who absolutely did not believe that an ant could talk, Amelia believed he could, although not having heard him talk, she wasn't sure.

"You know something? I never asked him. I should've. I will when he comes back. You know he comes and goes."

"Maybe he only lets children hear him. Then you could let me see him and he could talk to me."

Sir Rufus came back later that day.

"My sister, Amelia, wants to hear you talk. She thinks that maybe Mom and Dad can't hear you because only children can. Amelia's only eleven. Would you talk so she can hear?"

"I'm not allowed to."

"Why aren't you allowed to and who says you can't?"

"A Committee of the International Ant Congress sets the rules. One of those rules is that only children who are sick and must stay in the hospital or must stay in a room at home can hear me. Somebody like you who must stay in your room because you are ill is said to be quarantined."

"Why just kids like me?"

"The International Ant Congress knows how lonely sick children can be when they can't leave the hospital or their rooms, and our job is to keep them company, play games with them, tell them stories, and just be friends with them."

"What happens when I'm all better and can leave my room and go wherever I want?"

"You won't hear me anymore, and you won't remember that you ever heard me."

"What about my parents, my friends, and my doctors? I've told them I've heard you. Will they remember that?"

"Not after you're allowed to leave this room. They may remember you talking to an ant, but they won't remember you telling them that the ant talked to you."

"But we're friends now. I don't want to lose my friend when I get well. Couldn't we just talk once in a while, maybe not as often as we do now?"

"No. The Congress has very strict rules, and it makes no exceptions."

CHAPTER NINE
AMELIA

"Mom, do you think that the ant actually talks to Chet?"

"Of course not. Don't be silly. Animals don't talk."

"Well, I read an article that said dolphins are very intelligent and they can talk to their trainers."

"I read articles too. Dolphins don't talk. Trainers seem to know what they mean by body language or something like that. Dolphins have big brains. How big a brain can an ant have—if it's got one at all?"

"Why would Chet say that the ant spoke to him if it didn't? Is he making it all up?"

"Not exactly. See, he's lonely. Up there in his room all day by himself, he's made an imaginary friend. Lots of children have imaginary friends. They're usually make-believe children, not ants. Of course, imaginary friends are not real. While the child pretty well knows the friend isn't real, he or she treats it like it is real. Now, wash up, it's time for dinner."

"How do you know all that?"

Dad spoke up. "The child psychiatrist told us about imaginary friends. It's perfectly normal. Lots of kids have them, but they grow out of it. Just like Chet will. Now, do what your mother said and get ready for dinner."

Ordinarily, Chet, Amelia, and their parents ate dinner together, unless either Chet or Amelia were at sleepovers or away at camp or their father was on a business trip. That routine had been broken when Chet was quarantined and had to eat all his meals alone in his room.

"Mom," Amelia asked, "may I eat in my room, please?"

"Why do you want to do that? We always eat dinner together when we're all at home."

"We're not doing that now with Chet in his room. I just think he won't feel so all alone if I can call him and tell him that I'm also eating dinner in my room just like he is. It might cheer him up."

Mom wiped a tear from the corner of her eye. "That's very sweet of you, dear. You can do it tonight, but you can't make a practice of it. Chet's still going to have another few weeks in his room."

Amelia took her plate and her phone up to her room. "Hi Chet, I'm eating dinner in my room just like you're eating dinner in your room. We're eating the same food on the same plates, and if we look out of our windows, we can both see the oak tree in the front yard and Dad's car in the driveway. It's kinda fun."

"It may be fun once in a while, but it gets to be a real drag."

"Is Sir Rufus Ant there?"

"No, we played some Chinese checkers, and then he had to go somewhere. He'll be back in the morning."

"Mom told me that you said that Sir Rufus can only be heard by children who are sick and must stay in their rooms alone. I'd love to hear him talk, but I wouldn't want to be sick to make that happen. Want to play a game? I've got my computer open. You pick what you want to play."

CHAPTER TEN
THE ASK COMMITTEE

"What's the matter, Chet? You don't look very happy this bright and shiny morning." Sir Rufus had just appeared on Chet's computer screen.

"I'm not happy. Today's the first flag football game at school. We're playing Lackland, and I would be the quarterback. But instead, I'm stuck in this room, and I'm going to be here forever."

"You know that's not true, Chet. You'll be out of here very soon and back in the world. You know something? You're a very, very lucky boy."

"You think I'm lucky? Stuck in this room for months. Can't go anywhere. Can't play on the football team. Can't even walk up and down the stairs."

"Let me tell you about something that may change your mind. The International Ant Congress formed a special group a long time ago. That group is called 'Ants for Sick Kids,' or 'ASK' for short. Members of ASK go all over the world to help sick kids, kids who have to be quarantined, kept by themselves—away from people sometimes for much longer than you. Many times, we see children in very poor and sometimes dangerous places in parts of Africa, in Syria, in Iraq, and lots of other places. Those kids don't have computers and TVs. They don't have wealthy parents who get them electronic games and expensive devices that let them talk to and see their friends and family. Some of them have nothing."

Chet looked down and spoke more softly. "I'm sorry. I wasn't thinking. I didn't know. How do you talk to those kids in all those countries? I bet most of them can't speak English."

"Ants in ASK can speak whatever language the kids in the different countries speak."

"Did you have to go to school to learn all these languages? That must take forever."

"No, we didn't have to go to school. When we go to a country, we just automatically find that we can speak the language of the people of the country."

"How do you help kids who don't have computers or TVs or games or even books? You wouldn't have anything to help them with."

"Yes we do. There's more to helping kids than just with things. We talk with them, tell them stories, and make up games that don't need any devices; we even sing to them and have them sing with us. We do lots of things that don't need anything other than kindness and caring."

"I guess not being able to play against Lackland is not that important."

"Yes, it's important. It's just that there are other things in life that are more important."

CHAPTER ELEVEN
BWANA CHANGU

Weeks went by. Chet kept up with his classes and did all his homework. He still went to class in his pajamas most of the time, and sometimes he would play Rontoona with Sir Rufus. Chet had learned the game so well that he often won. It was a lot of fun, and it was not the only thing Sir Rufus told him about. Sometimes Chet would listen for hours while Sir Rufus told him about all the places he had been to in Europe, Asia, Africa, and the Americas. He told him about all the children he had visited and helped in all of those places. He told him about how the people lived, what schools the kids went to, if any, and what games they played; many were the same as American kids played, and some were different.

Chet had not seen or spoken to Sir Rufus for several days. When he then appeared, Chet asked him where he had been.

"I've been to Africa to see a girl who had recovered from her illness and was back in school and out playing with her friends."

"I thought you told me that when a child was all better and was able to leave her room, she would not remember anything about you."

"That's right. That little girl doesn't remember anything about me and never will hear me speak again."

"Why did you go to see her, then?"

"We have to make a final report to ASK when the children we have been helping are better and not required to stay in their rooms anymore. We tell ASK how long we were with the child when he or she was ill, what types of games and talks we had, and when the assignment was over. We also tell ASK how the child is doing after he or she is able to leave the room. They need all of that for their records. We also tell ASK about such things as what names the children made up for us, if they did. I'll tell them that you called me 'Sir Rufus Ant.'"

"Did the little girl that you just saw in Africa give you a name?"

"Yes she did. She called me 'Bwana Changu.' That's 'Mr. Ant' in Swahili, which is a language spoken in that part of the world."

"How is it possible for you to get from here to Africa and back in two or three days? It would take you that long or more for you to crawl from my tablet to the front door."

"I don't get from one place to another place many miles away by crawling or walking. I'm told where to go and I close my eyes, think about where I'm to go, and say a few words, which are like a password that someone might use to log into a computer or smart phone. Then I open my eyes, and I'm there. Same thing coming back."

"Can all ants do that?"

"Oh no. Just a few who have had special training in caring for lonely children and who work for ASK."

CHAPTER TWELVE
THE 'END' OF SIR RUFUS

Several days later, Chet and Sir Rufus were playing another game of Rontoona when his mother came in.

"Mom, I'm beating Sir Rufus at Rontoona."

"That's wonderful!" But she sounded more exasperated than pleased. While she was glad that Chet was occupied with an imaginary friend, his constant talking about this nonexistent insect was beginning to wear on her.

"I've got to clean in here. This room is a mess. You've left stuff all over the place." She picked up a book that was lying on the floor, and before Chet could say or do anything, she quickly put it down on a table beside the bed. Chet ran over, grabbed the book, turned it over, and screamed.

"You've killed him! You've killed Sir Rufus!" Chet fell on the floor, sobbing uncontrollably.

"I'm sorry. I didn't mean it. I didn't know he was on the table. Don't be so upset. He was only an ordinary ant. I'll get rid of him."

"No, I'll do it," Chet said between sobs. "I'll bury him."

"Okay, I'll come back later and clean the room."

After she left, Chet sat for hours, looking at the poor crushed body of Sir Rufus. "I didn't know him long. Not nearly long enough, but he was one of my best friends." Chet got up and walked around the room. "He wasn't ONE of my best friends. He was my VERY BEST FRIEND, and now he's gone."

Chet thought about getting a box and burying Sir Rufus in it. Maybe he'd get Amelia to make some sort of marker and write something on it. Amelia was good at drawing and stuff like that.

It was starting to get dark, but Chet continued to gaze at Sir Rufus through now-reddened eyes. Suddenly, he thought he saw a slight movement. He rubbed his eyes. He must be imagining things. The fading light was playing tricks. The movement became more pronounced. Chet couldn't believe what he was seeing.

Slowly, over a period of several minutes, Sir Rufus's body gradually got back its original shape. Then he stood up, shook himself, and turned toward Chet.

"I'm okay. Really I am. You can't kill us. At least not until our time is up, and mine won't be up for a long, long time. So, dry your eyes."

Chet had seen and heard some magical things about Sir Rufus—being able to speak, to travel the world, to talk in languages he had never heard before, and lots of other things—but nothing like this.

Chet shouted, "Mom, Mom, Sir Rufus is alive! I'm talking to him! He's fine!"

His mother came running up the stairs. "I'm so happy for you." She truly was pleased, not because she believed anything about Sir Rufus, but because Chet's unhappiness had deeply saddened her, and now he sounded like his old self. "Now, finish your homework," she said gently. "You can play with Sir Rufus later."

CHAPTER THIRTEEN
THE ENVELOPE

"You know, Amelia, I was just thinking about what Sir Rufus said to me about my never hearing him again after I get well and leave this room. He said that I won't even remember him ever talking to me and everybody who I told about him talking to me or who somehow knew about it also wouldn't remember anything. He said if I did remember but couldn't ever hear him again, it would make me sad."

"Well, would it?"

"Yes, I guess it would, but I would still like to remember at least something about him: that I called him Sir Rufus Ant, that he told me stories, and that we played games, and all about the ASK ants."

"Maybe you could write some things on a piece of paper about all the conversations with Sir Rufus and everything else about him and what he told you. You could put it in an envelope and only open it after you were all better and had left the room and had no memory of Sir Rufus."

"That's a great idea, Amelia! I'm gonna do it."

That afternoon he sat down and wrote the following:

I'VE BEEN SICK AND WAS NOT ALLOWED TO LEAVE MY ROOM FOR A LONG TIME. I MET AN ANT WHO APPEARED ON MY LAPTOP. I CALLED HIM SIR RUFUS ANT. HE SPOKE TO ME ABOUT A LOT OF THINGS AND WE PLAYED GAMES AND TALKED AND HE REALLY HELPED ME THROUGH THE LONELINESS OF BEING ALL BY MYSELF IN MY ROOM FOR A LONG TIME. HE TOLD ME THAT HE WORKED FOR "ASK" WHICH WAS SHORT FOR "ANTS FOR SICK KIDS." HE AND OTHER ANTS WENT ALL OVER THE WORLD FOR THESE CHILDREN AND BY SOME SORT OF MAGIC COULD SPEAK THEIR LANGUAGE EVEN THOUGH THE ANTS HAD NEVER LEARNED THOSE LANGUAGES. SIR RUFUS HAS TOLD ME THAT ONCE I'M WELL AND LEAVE MY ROOM NEITHER I NOR ANYONE ELSE WILL REMEMBER HIM OR OUR TALKS. I'M WRITING THIS SO I WILL REMEMBER SOME THINGS.

Chet put the note in an envelope and wrote "Private and Confidential" on the outside.

When his mother came into his room with his dinner, he said, "Mom, will you keep this envelope in a very safe place and give it to me when I'm better and I leave this room?"

"What's in it?"

"I'll tell you when I open it. Please don't lose it."

Chapter Fourteen
Goodbye Sir Rufus

Dr. Garcia had just finished examining Chet. "Well, Chet, the great day has arrived. You're now better and able to leave your room I know it's been a long haul for you, but you've been very brave."

"I had help."

"I know your mom and dad, Amelia, and your friends all pitched in."

"There was also someone else."

"Well, good. I'll have your mom and dad bring you into the office in a month or so, just to see how you're doing."

His mom said, "Come on downstairs."

"I will in a minute. There's something I have to do."

The door closed and Sir Rufus appeared. "Well, this is it, Chet. I'm so happy you are well and ready to pick up your life. I hope the school football team will do better with you back with them. As soon as you walk out of that door, you and your relatives, your friends, your doctors, and anybody else will have absolutely no memory of me and our times and talks together."

Chet started to tear up, and he blurted out, "I love you. I really do. I never could have got through this without you."

"I love you too. You won't remember me, but I'll remember you, always. Goodbye, dear Chet." And with those last words in his ears, Chet walked out of the room and down the stairs.

Dad, Mom, Amelia, and Chet were sitting at dinner—the first time they had all been together at the table in months. There was laughter and a few tears.

"Oh Chet, I almost forgot that envelope you wanted me to keep for you and give you when you were able to leave your room. I'll go get it," Mom said, and she did.

"Here it is, all safe and sound. Now we'll find out why you wouldn't tell me what was in it before, and why it's so mysterious."

"I don't know what it is."

"Well, open it, and we'll all find out."

Chet tore open the envelope and pulled out a single piece of paper. He looked at it, perplexed. He turned it over and then held it up to the light. He searched in the envelope to see if there was anything else in there. There wasn't.

"Well, what does it say?"

"Nothing. It's a blank piece of paper."

"Why did you put a blank piece of paper in an envelope and make me think it was something important?"

Chet was looking confusedly at the blank piece of paper.

"I don't remember anything about it. Amelia, do you want to play Rontoona?"

"What's that? I never heard of it."

Chet looked puzzled. "I never heard of it, either. I don't know what made me say it. I must have read it somewhere. Forget it. Let's play chess."

Upstairs, Chet's bedroom was now dark and quiet, the silence broken only by an occasional faint laugh from downstairs. The door was closed and the drapes drawn. The only light in the room came from his computer. For a few seconds, a tiny ant sat motionless in the center of the screen. It whispered, "Have a great life, Chet." It then moved slowly to the edge of the screen and disappeared.

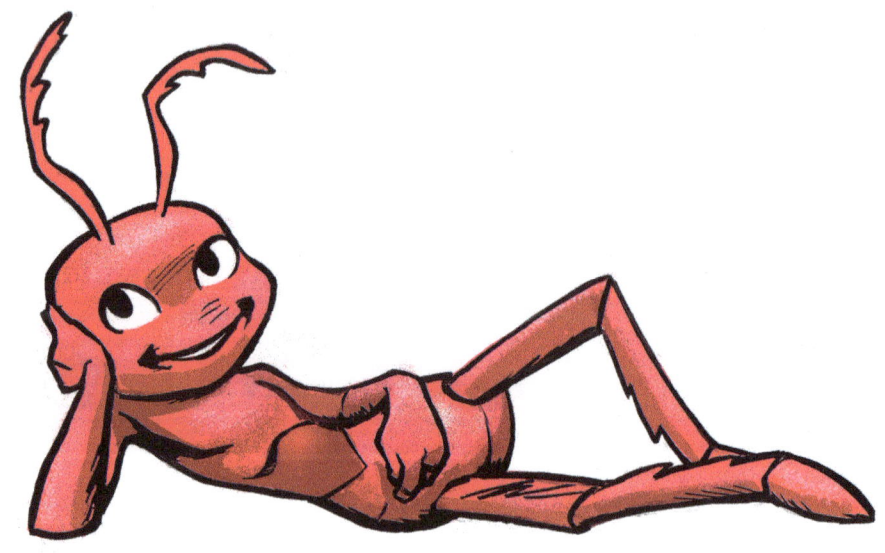

www.ingramcontent.com/pod-product-compliance
Lightning Source LLC
Chambersburg PA
CBHW061145010526
44118CB00026B/2875